So You're
80!

Mike Haskins & Clive Whichelow

summersdale

SO YOU'RE 80!

Summersdale Publishers Ltd
46 West Street
Chichester
West Sussex
PO19 1RP
UK

www.summersdale.com

Printed and bound in China

ISBN: 978-1-84953-021-7

Substantial discounts on bulk quantities of Summersdale books are available to corporations, professional associations and other organisations. For details contact Summersdale Publishers by telephone: +44 (0) 1243771107, fax: +44 (0) 1243 786300 or email: nicky@summersdale.com.

TO...

FROM...

Other titles in this series:

So You're 30!
So You're 40!
So You're 50!
So You're 60!
So You're 70!
So You're a Grandparent!
So You're Having a Mid-life Crisis!
So You're Retired!
So It's Your Anniversary!
So It's Your Birthday!

INTRODUCTION

Wow! Gosh! No, never! You, 80? You can't be! Well I suppose you must be or you wouldn't be reading this book, would you?

At one time 80 was quite old, but not any more. No, 80 is the new 70. Unlike Greece, you still have all your marbles; you may even still be playing marbles. You enjoy life to the full, though you may have begun to cut back a bit on the wilder side of things.

These days, your idea of an extreme sport might be getting the top off the ketchup or simply standing up straight after a prolonged session in a comfy chair, although it comes to us all eventually.

But, hey, reaching 80 is something to celebrate! So pop open a bottle of something fizzy, throw away all those preconceived ideas about what 80-year-olds should be like and have a whale of a time! You're just 20 for the fourth time round!

REASONS TO BE CHEERFUL

People will comment on how marvellous
you are even if you've simply walked to
the corner shop unaided

All those times when you wished you
had a moment to sit down, relax and
contemplate life – now you've got it!

You could join the Rolling Stones
and not look out of place

WHY 80 REALLY
ISN'T THAT OLD

It is said that the oldest turtle lived to
be 250 – in turtle years you're
not even middle aged!

You're still more than forty years younger than the oldest person ever to have lived!

You're just a nipper compared to some of those characters in the Bible (Methuselah – 969, Noah – 950, Adam – 930, Deborah – 130 etc.)

WHY 80 IS THAT OLD

If you were a car you'd have been crushed years ago

If you were a bottle of wine, you'd be even older than some of the finest vintages on earth

The glare from your birthday candles
can be seen from space

If you were a house, you'd be in need
of extensive modernisation and new
plumbing (which ironically you
feel you require anyway)

GIVEAWAYS THAT WILL TELL PEOPLE YOU ARE OVER 80

Your house has more support rails than a funfair full of white-knuckle rides

You've got a King George VI coronation mug on the sideboard

Very few people seem willing to accept a lift when they find out you're driving

CULTURE CONVERTER

When speaking with people younger
than yourself it's no good talking about
things that happened before they were
born; they won't have a clue what you're
on about. So here is a handy culture
converter to translate your cultural
reference points to their equivalent.

CATEGORY	YOUNGSTERS	MIDDLE AGED	80s
Favourite eating out experiences in youth	Happy Meal at McDonald's	Wimpy Burger at a Wimpy Bar	Spam sandwiches in the air raid shelter
Memorable beaches	Florida	Brighton	Normandy on D-Day
Sexy film star pin-ups	Zac Efron and Vanessa Hudgens	Steve McQueen and Raquel Welch	George Formby and Gracie Fields
Music technology enjoyed when young	Music downloads on MP3 player	Enormous booming stereo hi-fi system	Wind up 78 rpm gramophone

WHY IT'S GREAT TO BE 80

You can be as rude as you like and
people will just think you're
'a bit of a character'

You can refer to almost anyone as
being 'wet behind the ears'
and/or a 'whippersnapper'

That money you saved for a rainy day
can now be spent – hooray!

NEW MEASURES OF SUCCESS
FOR 80-YEAR-OLDS

Managing to get a whole hour's sleep
between nocturnal trips to the loo

Watching an entire film
without nodding off

Remembering where you parked
your mobility scooter

Eating a toffee without gluing your
dentures together for the rest of the day

NOW YOU'RE 80 THE FOLLOWING WILL BE YOUR NATURAL ENEMIES

People who speak quietly

Any technological device
introduced since the 1970s

Stairs

Small print

Small print warning of stairs

THINGS YOU ARE NOW LIKELY TO HAVE IN YOUR HOME

A seven-day organiser box
for all your pills

The phone number of an
emergency chiropodist

A mechanical device for grabbing things off high shelves (or low floors)

Tartan rugs to keep your legs warm

At least one room that looks like a
small museum of antique china

THINGS YOU SHOULD NOT HAVE IN YOUR HOME

Any pet larger than a cat – because at
80 you won't be able to cope with it

A home tattooing kit – it's
very difficult to write neatly
on a wrinkly surface

A stunt circuit – on which you can perform jumps and tricks on your mobility scooter

The game Twister – that really would be asking for trouble

YOUTH ENHANCERS TO AVOID

Too much make-up –
especially if you're a man

Plastic surgery – at your age you would
probably have to have Bakelite
surgery instead

Botox – being forgetful is bad enough but having a permanently blank expression will only make it worse

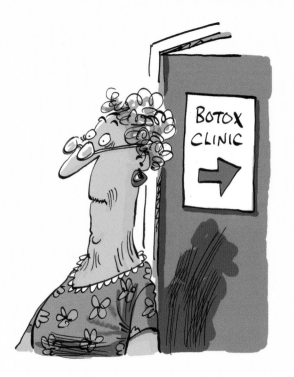

BOTOX
CLINIC
→

HOW TO BE PHILOSOPHICAL
ABOUT BEING 80

You're still only in double digits!

You may now be entering a state of great
spiritual enlightenment… alternatively
it might be that you've just
nodded off for a moment

If you think hitting 80 is bad,
consider the alternative

George Burns had just re-launched
himself as a movie star at 80,
Matisse was still painting at 84 and
Coco Chanel was still running
her fashion empire at 85

THINGS THAT WILL REALLY MAKE YOU FEEL OLD

Meeting some doddery old fool in the
pension queue and learning that
they're younger than you

Realising that being 80 years old means
you have been alive for over two
and a half billion seconds

Seeing a photograph of your family gathered round some ancient individual and then realising that it's you

Discovering that your life spans the entire history syllabus being taught at a local school

PHRASES YOU'LL FIND CREEPING INTO YOUR VOCABULARY

'Do I know you?'

'Speak up a bit will you?'

'Where are my pills?'

'I'm 80 you know!'

'Can you get this thing to work for me?'

WORDS OF WISDOM YOU CAN NOW SHARE WITH YOUR JUNIORS

'Sex is a vastly overrated pastime'

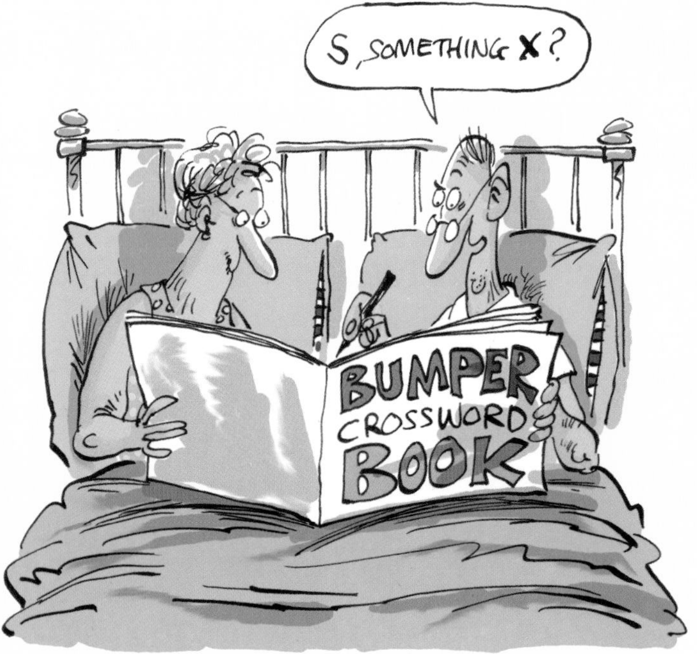
S, SOMETHING X?
BUMPER CROSSWORD BOOK

'We'd feed a family of six on a couple of powdered eggs and an Oxo cube'

'My first wage packet was £1 for a 48 hour week and it was still enough to buy myself my first car and have change left over'

WAYS YOU MAY START TO DESCRIBE YOUR AGE

'Only eleven and a half in dog years'

'Recently retired'

'I've been around the block a few times… and a bloomin' big block it was too!'

HOBBIES YOU PROBABLY SHOULDN'T CONSIDER TAKING UP

Speed dating (maybe slightly-slower-than-average dating instead)

Pole dancing

Any sport with the word 'extreme' in front of it – e.g. extreme tiddlywinks

Marathon running – it's exhausting enough just walking up the stairs these days

Kick-boxing
(unless it's with 90-year-olds)

WAYS FOR 80-YEAR-OLDS TO SURPRISE FRIENDS AND FAMILY

Announce you're marrying someone sixty years your junior who you've just met on match.com

Suddenly perform an impromptu display of high energy disco dancing for them

Announce your plan to do a sponsored parachute jump

YOUR NEW OUTLOOK ON LIFE

The spirit may still be willing but the flesh has become a real party pooper in recent years

You didn't get to this age without learning a thing or two – if only you could remember what they were

If all good things come to those who
wait, how much longer is
it going to take?!

THINGS YOU CAN DO THAT YOUNGSTERS CAN'T

Have a polite conversation
with a total stranger

Make a decent cup of tea

Get all the drugs you need
without breaking the law

Spell

Get through a whole day
without using the phone

Eat as much as you like
without putting on weight

STATISTICALLY SPEAKING

The hungry thirties, the roaring forties, the… er, nineteen fifties, the swinging sixties, you've seen 'em all come and go.

Congratulations! You're still here, going strong. What's your secret?

Could it be all the tea you've drunk? A modest five cups a day since you were five means you've glugged your way through 136,968 cups of the brown stuff – and we won't even mention the biccies.

Did you know that the population of
the world has more than trebled
since you were born?

No wonder there's always such a queue
at the post office on pension day.

Let's say you worked from 15 to 65, and now you're 80 you've been collecting the state pension for fifteen years. This means that in a couple of years you'll have got perhaps a third of your money back!

Add in free travel, all those free prescriptions, hearing aids, spectacles, dentures, hip replacements, and you may now be on the profit side!

Whatever disadvantages there may be in reaching 80, doesn't it make your heart soar to know that you've got one over on the tax man, the health service and everyone else who's been milking your wages for years?

Finally, heroically, and magnificently, you're beating the system! Well done!

PRODUCTS YOU'D LIKE TO SEE

Motorised scooters for two

Bionic replacement body parts
available on prescription

A walking frame with a built-in toilet
in case there isn't one around
while you're out

A walking stick with a cattle prod attachment to help clear your way through the crowds at the supermarket

Additional memory – well, if they can do it for computers...

GAMES FOR WICKED
80-YEAR-OLDS TO PLAY

Spin the Medicine Bottle

Guess Who's Not In My Will?

Trapping any visitors with endless cups
of tea until they have listened
to your entire life story

Lying very still until people look worried
then jumping up and shouting, 'Boo!'

Pretending to be deaf so you
don't have to respond to silly
comments from anyone

DOS AND DON'TS FOR 80-YEAR-OLDS

Do keep a panic alarm in case
you accidentally fall

Don't use it to call the emergency
services to help you reach the new
cornflakes packet on the top shelf

Do have a good laugh now and then

Don't do it alone in the high street –
people will think you're gaga

Do learn to slow down a bit

Don't do it when paying at a busy
supermarket checkout though

NEW YEAR'S RESOLUTIONS YOU MAY NOW ACTUALLY STICK TO

To cut down on all-night drinking binges
– unless it's Horlicks

To lose weight this year – unfortunately you might lose a bit more height as well

To stop gallivanting with members of the opposite sex – especially those frisky young 70-year-olds

To avoid smoking – mainly because a couple of packets of cigarettes costs about half your weekly pension

To make sure you see a bit more of the world – get your cataracts done

BEING 80 IS...

… having to decline all requests to join
the local acrobatic display team

THE
AMAZING
OCTO-
FLEXIES
★ ★

... counting your blessings instead of your calorie intake

... soldiering on and not dropping off

... learning to slow down without actually coming to a complete stop

... learning that 'pleasure' has a silent 'p'

AWARDS YOU THINK YOU SHOULD BE GIVEN

A literary and public speaking award for telling people the same stories over and over again without anyone ever saying, 'You've told us this one before'

An award in special recognition that you've survived so long on the measly pension they give you

A world land speed medal for getting to the downstairs toilet and back in just under ten minutes

THE UPSIDE OF BEING 80

You're at last about the right age to be
appointed as the new Pope

By now you must surely qualify
as a design classic

You have survived all the things that people always said weren't good for you, such as drinking, smoking and eating food that is two days past its sell-by date

Have you enjoyed this book?
If so, why not write a review on
your favourite website?

Thanks very much for buying
this Summersdale book.

www.summersdale.com